Festen

David Eldridge was born in Romford, Essex, in 1973 and began writing full time after graduating from Exeter University in 1995. His full-length plays include *Serving It Up* (Bush Theatre, 1996); *A Week with Tony* (Finborough Theatre, 1996); *Summer Begins* (RNT Studio and Donmar Warehouse, Four Corners Festival of New Writing, 1997); *Falling* (Hampstead Theatre, A Small Drop of Ink Festival of New Writing, 1999), and *Under the Blue Sky* (Royal Court Jerwood Theatre Upstairs, 2000), which in January 2001 was awarded the *Time Out* Live Award for Best New Play in the West End. His short plays include *Cabbage for, Tea, Tea, Tea!* (Exeter University, 1995), *Fighting for Breath* (Finborough Theatre, 1995), *Dirty* (Theatre Royal Stratford East, Young Voices, 1996) and *Thanks Mum* (Red Room and BAC, 1998). Television and short film includes *Killers* (BBC Choice) and *The Nugget Run* (Sixteenth Foyle Film Festival). Radio includes *Michael and Me* and *Stratford, Ilford, Romford and All Stations to Shenfield* (BBC Radio 4).

**Thomas Vinterberg, Mogens Rukov
and Bo hr. Hansen's**

Festen

adapted for the stage by

David Eldridge

Methuen Drama

Published by Methuen 2004

3 5 7 9 10 8 6 4 2

First published in 2004 by
Methuen Publishing Limited
215 Vauxhall Bridge Road
London SW1V 1EJ

Thomas Vinterberg, Mogens Rukov and Bo hr. Hansen have asserted
their rights under the Copyright, Designs and Patents Act, 1988,
to be identified as the authors of this work

Stage play of *Festen* copyright © 2004
Thomas Vinterberg, Mogens Rukov and Bo hr. Hansen

David Eldridge has adapted this work for performance
in the English language

Cover Photo: John Dolan / Getty Images

Methuen Publishing Limited Reg. No. 3543167

A CIP catalogue record for this book is available from
the British Library

ISBN 0 413 77438 4

Typeset by Country Setting, Kingsdown, Kent
Printed and bound in Great Britain by
Cox and Wyman Ltd, Reading, Berkshire

Caution

For Marla Rubin

For C

The author would like to thank Thomas Vinterberg, Mogens Rukov, Marla Rubin and Rufus Norris for their patience and their wise advice.

DE, February 2004

This stage adaptation of *Festen* received its World Premiere at the Almeida Theatre, London on 18 March 2004. The cast was as follows:

Christian	Jonny Lee Miller
Michael	Tom Hardy
Helene	Claire Rushbrook
Mette	Lisa Palfrey
Helge	Robert Pugh
Else	Jane Asher
Helmut	Michael Thomas
Poul	Sam Cox
Grandfather	Sam Beazley
Pia	Ruth Millar
Kim	Gary Oliver
Lars	Andrew Maud
Gbatokai	Patrick Robinson

Direction Rufus Norris
Design Ian MacNeil
Costume Design Joan Wadge
Lighting Jean Kalman
Music Orlando Gough
Sound Paul Arditti
Fight Director Terry King

Marla Rubin is delighted to be co-producing the Almeida Theatre Company's production of *Festen* as her first theatrical venture. As well as producing for film and television, Marla Rubin has introduced the groundbreaking initiative of bringing the Danish film collective Dogme 95 to the stage.

Note

The playscript that follows was correct at time of going to press, but may have changed during rehearsal.

Festen

Characters

Christian
Michael
Helene
Mette
Helge
Else
Helmut
Poul
Grandfather
Pia
Kim
Lars
Gbatokai
Michael and **Mette's Little Girl**

Place

A large house in the countryside, Denmark

Note

/ indicates overlapping dialogue

1.1

Christian *stands alone with a bag. He feels uneasy. Pause. Michael and Mette's* **Little Girl** *enters.* **Christian** *notices her.* **Michael** *enters with a suitcase.*

Michael   It's my big brother.

He takes a few steps and studies **Christian**. **Mette** *enters, struggling with their cases.*

Jesus, Christian! Why didn't you say he was here?

Mette   As if I knew he was here.

Michael *drops his case.*

Michael   Have I got to do every fucking thing myself?

Mette   Oh relax! Jesus Christ.

Michael *embraces him.*

Michael   Bloody hell, Christian! Jesus Christ, man.

He attacks him in jest, kisses him, grapples with him and climbs on his back.

Jesus Christ, you look so good I could climb on you now. Jesus, look at you! I could fuck you!

Christian *laughs and notices* **Mette**. **Michael** *lets him go.*

Christian   You're high-spirited today. Hi. Hi there.

Michael   It's been a long time. You see this man here? You see this man? He's walked all the way from Paris! My big brother!

Michael *laughs and hugs* **Christian** *again. A slight pause.*

Christian   No, only from the station. I can help you with the cases, if you want?

Michael   No, no, no – me and you need to talk. You two take the luggage. Go on. Hop it.

Mette *notices* **Michael**'s *suitcase.*

Mette   You want me to lug everything, do you?

Michael   What's your problem today? What's the matter with you?

Christian *makes a move towards the bag but* **Michael***'s glare halts him.* **Michael** *jabs* **Christian** *playfully in the back.*

Has a man got to do every fucking thing himself?

Mette   Michael.

Michael   Go and get the rest of the bags, otherwise you can go home. I'm speaking to Christian. Now. Go on. I'm speaking to my brother, for fuck's sake. Go on.

Mette   Oh, for God's sake shut up, Michael!

Michael   Come on. We're late.

Mette   Arsehole!

Mette *considers it and then disappears with the* **Little Girl***.* **Christian** *meets his brother's eye.*

Michael   Don't take any notice of her. She's completely fucking hysterical.

Michael *and* **Christian** *turn around and inspect the room.*

Where's Dad?

Michael *shouts.*

Hello?

Christian   I think he's out hunting somewhere. Don't you?

Christian *looks around.* **Lars** *enters.*

Michael   What's your name?

Lars   Lars.

Michael   Okay, Mads. Listen to me. I have this problem with new people. I want you to know that. Just so you know. I'd like you to know that.

Lars   Hello.

Christian Hi.

Michael Who do you think we are?

Lars *is about to speak when* **Michael** *cuts him off.*

This is Christian. Do you know who he is?

Lars *is again about to speak when* **Michael** *cuts him off again.*

This is my brother. You know this man has got two restaurants in Paris. Seriously.

Lars Of course.

Michael And I've got a café in Copenhagen.

A slight pause.

We were brought up here. We know how you're supposed to treat guests here. If you want to be on the ball, you'll keep an eye on who's who. Am I being clear enough for you, Mads? Do you understand me? Why don't you give us our old rooms and we won't mention any of this to the old man.

Lars I'm afraid you're not invited.

Michael What did you say?

Lars I said you're not invited.

Lars *allows himself a small smile.*

Michael What do you mean, I'm not invited?

Lars I said you're not invited.

Michael What do you fucking mean, I'm not invited?

Lars What I say, Mr Hansen.

Lars *allows himself a further small smile. A slight pause.*

Christian Please. Michael Hansen.

Lars I'm sorry. Your father informed me that Michael isn't invited.

Michael Now listen here, Mads.

Lars   Lars. My name is Lars.

Christian *smiles. He's enjoying* **Michael**'*s discomfort.*

Michael   Okay, Lars. Things got out of hand last year. I know that.

A slight pause.

I had too much to drink.

A slight pause.

When I have one too many, I go a bit mad. Now we need to sort something out, don't we? I'm here with my wife and my daughter. All I want to know is, is there a room for me, or isn't there?

Lars   There isn't a room.

Michael   Well, what do you suggest we do? Pitch a tent and camp in the fucking woods?

Lars *allows himself a small smile.* **Michael** *looks at* **Christian** *and then* **Lars**. **Michael** *explodes.*

I want to talk to my father! Now!

Lars   He's out shooting.

Michael   It's your job to sort something out. It's your job to work this sort of thing out! I don't know why I've got to put up with this shit, Mads. This is your job!

Christian   Lars. Michael. Lars?

Lars   Yes?

Christian   Find them a room. I'll talk to Dad about it.

Michael   I'll have the small room.

Christian   He can have that room.

Michael   It's always empty. No one ever stays in there. Give me that one.

Michael *is already on his way out.* **Lars** *holds up a key.*

Lars   Don't you need this?

Lars *hands* **Christian** *his key.*

Christian   Is my sister here?

Lars   No, she hasn't arrived yet.

Mette *and the* **Little Girl** *struggle in with the rest of their baggage. The* **Little Girl** *dumps her bags and runs to her father.*

Mette   This is the last time I do this, Michael!

Michael   Shut up and stop moaning, will you?

Mette   Can't you please at least for once be a gentleman and help me!

Michael *considers it.*

Michael   Lars, take the bags down to our room. Take them all down to our room, will you? You go with him, Mette. I'll be down.

Mette *is unhappy.*

Michael   And fill the car up, will you? Put some petrol in the car. I know nothing much happens here, but I want to leave tomorrow morning. You should take a word of my advice and buck your ideas up.

Lars *tosses the key to* **Michael** *and he allows himself a small smile.*

Michael   Did you see that? When the workers hear from their betters – they listen.

Lars *doesn't move.* **Michael** *grudgingly picks up the bags and they exit.* **Christian** *checks his watch.* **Lars** *sees he wants to be alone, nods to* **Christian** *and exits in a different direction.* **Christian** *thinks. Pause.*

Helene *enters. She is carrying a shoulder bag and is excited.*

Helene   Hi, Christian! Hi, baby, how are you? Oh, Jesus. Hi, darling, hi. Thanks for meeting me! That's sweet!

They embrace. She looks closely at **Christian**.

You haven't been drinking, have you?

A slight pause.

Christian   No. Not today.

Helene   It was a fantastic funeral, wasn't it?

Christian   Yeah. It was beautiful.

A slight pause.

Michael *enters.*

Helene   What are you doing here?

A slight pause.

Michael   What am I doing here?

Helene *is unhappy. A slight pause.*

What am I doing here? You're asking me what I'm doing here.

Helene   If you can't be bothered to come to the funeral, you shouldn't bother to come to your father's party either. I'm asking you what you're doing here? You're not invited.

Pause.

Michael   I think you should mind your own fucking business.

Pause.

Especially when you're always the last one to come traipsing in.

Helene   You know what, Michael? I don't mind what you do. But I do mind what you don't do. You don't even bother to come to your own sister's funeral. You don't bother to ring me on my birthday. You don't bother to pay me back the money you owe me. You don't give a shit.

Helene *smiles and approaches* **Michael**, *who retreats.*

Michael She's starting again, you hear this, Christian? She's off again.

Helene I'm off again?

Michael I don't need this, Christian. You know I don't need this? I think I'm going to go home. I'm going home, Christian. I've had enough of this shit already.

Helene What a brilliant idea. Go on then. Bye, Michael.

Christian You can borrow my bike.

A slight pause.

Michael I can't be fucking bothered to stand here and listen to her shit.

Christian Be quiet now. It's always the same.

Michael Yeah, be quiet!

Helene Well done, Michael! Big man! Just like Christian! Who's a clever boy? Who's a clever boy, eh, Michael? Are you?

Michael *gently kicks* **Helene***'s bottom.* **Michael** *and* **Helene** *fight and jostle each other like children.* **Michael** *slaps* **Helene** *on her behind and she screams as she tries to get away from him.*

Christian Stop it!

Helene Stop that! Leave me alone!

Michael *picks* **Helene** *up and throws her over his shoulder. She screams as he spins her round.*

Put me down, Michael! Put me down! Don't do that!

Michael *puts her down.*

Helene Come here, you bastard!

Michael *runs out, chased by* **Helene***.* **Christian** *thinks. He steels himself.*

1.2

Else *enters. She is almost ready for the party.* **Helge** *enters with a bottle and two glasses.* **Christian** *studies them.* **Helge** *and* **Else** *have some distance between them.*

Else   Hi, darling.

She gives him a hug.

How lovely that you could make it in the end.

Christian   Hi, Mum.

He kisses her. A slight pause.

You look beautiful.

Else   Thank you.

A slight pause.

Go and see your father. Look, he's waiting for you. And don't forget to say happy birthday.

Christian *goes over to his father.* **Else** *watches them.*

Christian   Hi, Dad. Happy birthday.

Helge   Thank you.

A slight pause.

Listen, there's something I want to tell you.

A slight pause.

Do you want a cognac?

Christian   No, thanks.

A slight pause.

Helge   It's rather important, actually. It's something I've been thinking about for a few days.

Christian   Okay.

Helge   It's very important to me. That I tell you now. Are you listening?

Helge *is deadly serious. Silence.*

Two prostitutes are sitting on a train.

Helge *chortles.* **Christian** *can't help but laugh.*

Don't you stand there and laugh at your dad on his birthday! Who do you think you are, eh? I'm going to have to tell your mother about this. Really I am. Else.

Else   I'm waiting for you two.

Helge   He's standing here laughing in my face. Look at him.

Else   Christian, you mustn't do that. You know how seriously your father takes himself.

Helge *isn't happy about this remark.*

Else   Hurry up. Come on.

Christian   We could always just stay, in here, and tell each other a few jokes? The others can wait.

Helge   Yes, that's right. Bugger them.

A slight pause.

All I feel like doing is staying here with you.

A slight pause.

How are things? How are you?

Else *shakes her head and smiles. She exits.*

Christian   I'm fine.

A slight pause.

Things are good. We've moved to Lyon now. I'm opening a restaurant there.

A slight pause.

Helge   I think you're doing very well, son. I read the newspapers. I think you really are. You're not half-asleep are you, boy? And what about that girl? Eh? Can't you have a baby with her and come back home?

A slight pause.

Christian   Actually, she's having a baby with someone else. She's a good friend of mine.

Helge   Well, then, we'll have to find you another lady, won't we?

A slight pause.

I'm getting older and I like to have my family around me. Then there's your mother.

Christian   What's the matter with Mum?

Helge   She's fed up with my jokes now.

Christian   I can see why.

Helge   What's wrong with them? There's no respect any more, is there? How are things?

Else *enters.* **Pia**, *a waitress, follows not far behind with a tray of empty glasses.*

Helge   Pia, have you got a boyfriend?

Pia *smiles.*

Else   Come on.

Helge   We're coming. Come on, Christian.

Christian *stands.* **Helge** *stops.*

Helge   Christian?

Christian   Yes?

Helge   There's one more thing. Do you think you could say a few words about your sister this evening?

A slight pause.

I can't manage it.

A slight pause.

I'll stand there blubbing.

Christian   Actually, I've written something.

Helge Have you? Well done.

A slight pause.

Christian Yeah.

Helge You're wonderful, son. Wonderful.

Helge *walks towards* **Else**. *He studies* **Pia** *for a moment. She's embarrassed.*

Christian Michael's here.

Helge Is he? Well, I suppose I'd better go and talk to him, hadn't I? Tell me something. Pia, my girl – are you married?

Else Helge.

Pia No.

Helge Oh yes – that's right.

Helge *gives* **Christian** *the cognac, nods to* **Pia** *and exits with* **Else**.

Pia Hi, Christian.

Christian Hello.

They look at each other.

Pia Where are you staying?

Christian In my old room. Why?

Pia I need to borrow your bath. Can I use your bath?

He gives her his room key. She nods to him.

See you later, then.

Christian See you later.

Pia *exits.* **Christian** *watches her go.*

1.3

Christian *is alone.* **Helene** *and* **Lars** *look at the room. There is a bed and a suitcase as well.* **Helene** *has a bag.*

Helene I don't know if this means anything to you. I don't know how sensitive you are.

Lars I'm sorry?

Helene I'm not making a fuss, but this is my sister's room. It's not really – satisfactory. But I suppose it's better than giving it to Christian.

Lars *is mortified.* **Mette** *enters and puts her dress on the bed. She is wearing a slip.*

Lars Would you like me to find you another room?

Helene *thinks about it.* **Michael** *enters holding his brown worn shoes. He is wearing underpants and socks.*

Michael I can't find them!

Mette They should be in the case, Michael.

Michael I've looked in the case. Do I have to do every fucking single thing myself?

Mette Relax, Michael. They must be here somewhere.

Michael *holds up his brown shoes.* **Pia** *enters.*

Michael Listen, I can't go to dinner in brown brogues. My dad will go fucking nuts.

Helene Christian and Linda were twins. Jesus, it's spooky.

Lars *looks around.* **Michael** *barks with rage.*

Pia Then, the third time I wanted to move to Copenhagen, Bettina H. moved in with him instead.

Mette Michael, I know they must be here somewhere.

Pia So I stayed here. It's been all right. I went to the park yesterday. I've been baking quite a lot. I'm making the pudding tonight. You're not listening to me.

Mette *and* **Michael** *look for the shoes.*

Christian Yes, I am.

Pia No, you're not. What did I say?

Christian That you're making the pudding tonight.

Pia Exciting, eh? I'm making the pudding.

Christian Yeah. Exciting.

Pia I'm the last one who's still here. You're all jet-setting off to Paris and everything. You're all so important now.

Michael *and* **Mette** *give up. A slight pause.*

Helene It happened in the bathroom. In there. Perhaps it'll be better if you find me another room?

Michael I've fucking looked everywhere, they're not here!

A slight pause.

Mette Shit, I think you forgot them.

Helene I'm getting a really bad feeling about this.

She hears a sound. **Pia** *is tearful.*

Michael Don't say that! Don't you fucking say that now, okay?

Mette I don't know what to do, Michael – you're bloody impossible!

Helene Did you hear that? I think she's in the bathroom.

Lars No. Please. She's – she's dead.

Helene *isn't convinced. A slight pause.*

Helene Let's have a look.

Lars I think we should go.

Helene Let's have a quick look.

Christian Don't cry.

Pia *cries.* **Christian** *goes to her.* **Helene** *puts her bag down and heads off.*

Michael   I'll tell you what you can do: go home, you go home and get them. We've got to go down to dinner in an hour. So you take the car and drive home and get them. You understand me?

Mette   There's no petrol in the car!

Michael   That's not my fucking problem, is it? I can't go down to my dad in my socks, can I?

Mette   You want me to go home now? Is that what you want? I can't do that, Michael! What the bloody hell do you think your parents will say?

Michael   I don't give a fuck what you can and can't do, but you know what, Mette? I'm not going to a dinner party in these shoes. Are you completely fucking mad?

Mette   Well, in the future, why don't you pack your own things? I packed your stuff, I packed my stuff, I packed up everything, and you leave me to do it all and then you insist that everything goes perfectly! If you're always so completely dissatisfied why don't you pack your own fucking shit in your own fucking suitcase!

He walks around her, working himself up. **Helene** *spots something.*

Helene   Jesus. There.

Lars   Where?

Helene   There. Pointing up.

Pia   I'm sorry.

Christian   Drink this.

Pia *takes the drink.* **Michael** *shouts at* **Mette** *while he chucks the contents of their suitcase onto the floor and wrinkles her dress. She shouts back at the same time.* **Michael** *grabs* **Mette** *by the hair and pulls her towards the contents of the case.* **Lars** *follows* **Helene**'s *eye-line up towards the ceiling.*

Michael   You're the one who packed the cases! You, you're the one who did it, not me! It's the same every fucking single time! All you've got to do is keep that shut and find my shoes!

Mette   You shut your fucking mouth, Michael! It's your bloody fault we had to come up here to see your stupid family!

Michael   You know what? I've fucking had it with you! It's my dad's birthday! It's my father's birthday! You listen – you don't tell me anything! All right? All right?

Mette *picks up her dress from the floor. It is completely wrinkled. She sinks to the floor and holds herself.* **Michael** *calms down.*

Pia   Tell me if you want me to go.

Christian   Weren't you going to take a bath?

A slight pause.

Helene   There, look.

Pia *takes her uniform off. She stands in front of* **Christian**. *She refers to her bra.*

Michael   Oh, and now I'm supposed to make things up with you, am I?

Mette   You don't have to comfort me.

Michael   Well then, stop that.

Mette *tries to smooth out her dress.* **Michael** *watches.*
Christian *lies on the bed. He watches* **Pia**.

Helene   And there. There's another arrow.

Pia   Can you undo me?

Christian   What do I do?

Pia *turns her back towards* **Christian**. **Lars**, *looking in the direction of* **Pia**, *thinks he sees something.*

Pia   Unhook the clasp.

Christian *takes her bra off.*

Pia   What do you think? I've still got a great arse.

Pia *turns back to* **Christian**, *letting him see her breasts.*

Are you just going to send me into the bath, Christian?

Christian *considers the question.*

Mette   I can't wear it like this, can I?

Michael   I got worked up. I'm sorry. Why don't we? We should lie down for five minutes.

Christian   I think so.

Pia   You're strange, Christian.

Christian   Am I?

Pia   You were the out-of-control one – you always got into fights. Now it's Michael. What happened, Christian? You can't even be bothered to make love to me. Do you think I'm too skinny?

Christian *looks at her, distracted.*

Pia   Christian, where are you?

Pia *picks up her uniform.* **Christian** *closes his eyes.* **Pia** *watches him.* **Michael** *clumsily tries to embrace* **Mette** *and to undo one of her buttons, but can't seem to get it undone.*

Mette   I thought you wanted to get ready?

Michael   Five minutes.

Michael *starts to take his clothes off.* **Mette** *follows suit.*

Mette   Sit down.

They sit down at a distance from each other and get undressed. Then **Mette** *lies down.* **Michael** *comes over and gets on top of her. They begin their intercourse, roughly.* **Helene** *spots something.*

Helene   Can you lie down on the bed? Just for a minute. If you lie down sometimes you can see something.

Lars *looks at the bed.* **Michael** *is having rough sex with* **Mette** *now.* **Christian** *is dozing.* **Pia** *dresses.*

Lars   You want me to lie down?

Helene   Sometimes the different perspective helps.

Lars *lies down.*

Helene   Look up. Look and see if you can see another little arrow or something like that. Like a wave. Or a fish. Or a bird. You know, like playing, 'Getting Hotter, Getting Colder'?

Lars   I'm not sure I understand the game.

Helene   She always played it. We're getting hotter. I'm sure.

She looks for a new sign. **Michael** *comes.* **Lars** *gets up.*

Look, she's drawn a little bird! Oh, how sweet. Like a sparrow.

A slight pause.

I can't bear this.

A slight pause.

There's an arrow. And there's another arrow. We're getting hotter and hotter but −

Lars *spots something up in the light.* **Michael** *leaves the room.*

Lars   Look, up there, up in the rim of the shade. There's something there.

Helene   Quickly!

Helene *gets the chair. She climbs up onto the back of the chair.* **Lars** *supports her. Up in the light she finds a letter.*

Here it is!

She climbs down and concentrates as she opens the letter. She walks a few steps away while she reads it.

Lars   What is it?

Helene *stops. She shakes her head and tears well up in her eyes.* **Lars** *tries to read the letter over her shoulder but she holds the letter against her bosom so he can't read it. She snaps.*

Helene Boo!

Lars Ah!

Lars *jumps with a start at* **Helene***'s bite.* **Pia** *looks up. So does* **Mette***.* **Michael** *comes back in.*

Michael What was that?

Mette *shakes her head.*

Helene It doesn't say anything. I'm sorry. Did I make you jump?

Lars No. Not at all.

Helene It doesn't say anything.

Pause.

There have always been ghosts in this house.

Michael *sits on the end of the bed, dressing.* **Pia** *looks at* **Christian** *and decides to leave him be.*

Lars Oh.

Helene I think I'll be all right in here.

Lars Are you sure?

Helene I'd like to stay in here, actually. Really. Thanks so much for your help. Thanks!

Lars Okay.

Lars *exits.* **Helene** *fishes in her bag. She cries.* **Mette** *gets up from the bed.* **Helene** *finds a tube of painkiller tablets, empties the tube into her bag, rolls the letter up and stuffs it down the tube.* **Pia** *exits.* **Helene** *puts the tube back in her bag.* **Mette** *goes out.* **Helene** *thinks and then she goes and lies down on the other side of the bed. A slight pause.*

Helge *enters and watches from the distance. He has Michael's* **Little Girl** *with him, a hand on her shoulder. He notices* **Christian** *on one side of the bed,* **Michael** *sitting dressing at the end of the bed and* **Helene** *on the other side of the bed.*

Helge   Quietly. That's it. While the coast is clear.

The **Little Girl** *bangs two pot lids together like a pair of cymbals.* **Christian**, **Michael** *and* **Helene** *look at their father with a start.*

Helge   Can I see your passports, your tickets and any other relevant travel documents?

Helge *smiles and the* **Little Girl** *runs and jumps up and down on the bed.*

2.1

Helge, **Else**, **Christian**, **Michael**, **Helene**, **Mette**, *Michael's* **Little Girl**, **Grandfather**, **Helmut** *and* **Poul** *are at a large dining table before the first course has been served. A place next to* **Helene** *remains empty. They all stand.* **Lars**, *the chef,* **Kim**, *and* **Pia** *stand at a respectful distance from the table, waiting to serve. All wear formal evening dress.* **Helmut** *leads everyone in a Danish birthday song.*

All
    It's Daddy's birthday.
    Oh yes it is and it is today
    It's Daddy's birthday
    Oh yes it is and it is today
    And now you'll hear how loud we sing
    And now you'll hear how loud we sing
    Tra la la la la
    Tra la la la la

N.B. The song is repeated three times exchanging 'sing', for 'clap' and then 'whistle'. The song ends with **Michael**.

Michael   And the sound of the sea.

They all make a 'ssshhh' sound. There is great applause and cheers and all sit, leaving only **Helmut** *on his feet.* **Helene** *glances at* **Christian** *before she takes her seat.*

Helmut   It's a great honour for me to be here this evening. Helge and Else with their usual great style welcome us here to another celebration. Everyone here knows I came here fresh-faced from Cologne, the Ruhr, the steelworks, and I started out washing the dishes in one of Helge's restaurants. Yet this evening I stand before you as his Managing Director. Helge is still going strong, a man of steel. I thank you for that my friend, for everything – with my deepest gratitude. Helge, my friend, my Danish father, the floor is yours.

They all applaud, as **Helmut** *sits and* **Helge** *stands. A slight pause.*

Helge   When I look at all of you I can remember very clearly the years that have passed by and all the things that have happened to us.

Christian *drinks. A slight pause.*

Helge   Turning sixty isn't anything exceptional in itself. For me, it feels like only yesterday we finalised the negotiations for taking over this magnificent place.

A slight pause.

It might have been yesterday that we first walked up the steps from the drive – my darling wife, Else, Helene, Michael and the twins. The twins. A day as hot as today. Wasn't it, darling?

Else *nods. A slight pause.*

Helge   Christian and Linda. They were – thrilled.

Christian *nods to his father to continue. A slight pause.*

Helge   All of us were ready to fill these beautiful rooms with our laughter. We were so – we were so full of – expectation.

Helge*'s voice cracks.*

I can't – I'll stop there. That's enough. I hope that you all enjoy this evening. Now, let's have something to eat, shall we? Let's eat.

There is gentle applause and **Else** *clasps* **Helge***'s hand as he sits.* **Kim** *exits and* **Lars** *and* **Pia** *begin to serve the first course, soup. They continue right through the scene. A slight pause.*

Helmut   It was a beautiful funeral.

Pause.

Grandfather   I'll probably say something later and it won't be anything for the ears of small girls.

Else   I hope that you can behave yourself, Grandfather.

Grandfather   Thanks very much!

Helene No, she's right.

Grandfather No, thanks very much!

Michael I know where I get it from.

Michael *laughs and turns to* **Mette** *with a grin.* **Mette** *isn't amused and deliberately spills some water into his lap. He gasps.*

Are you fucking mad?

As the guests are served they begin to eat.

Mette Shut up, Michael.

Grandfather And you dear. I'll probably say something later but it won't be anything for the ears of small girls.

Helene Oh – Grandad.

Grandfather What's your name?

Mette Mette. M–E–T–T–E.

Poul *loosens his top button.*

Poul Is it hot in here or is it me? It's very hot in here.

Helene I think it is hot.

Helmut It's great to see you all again. We had a lovely time last year.

Poul I think we're in for a great party!

Michael Poul, you old bastard, are we going shooting again?

Poul I think we should wait until I'm feeling a bit more hopeful.

Pause.

Helmut Your father asked me to be the sort of master of ceremonies. You don't mind, do you, Christian?

Christian Of course not.

Michael How's it all going, Poul?

Poul Dreadful, as it happens. The heat's making me feel hopelessly depressed. I feel like throwing myself from the bridge.

Long pause.

Helge Helmut has always done everything he possibly can for us.

Helmut But, of course, Helge.

Helge And now, Michael, I've been asked to ask you what you think about the lodge?

A slight pause.

Michael The lodge?

Helmut Yes.

Helge *notices* **Christian** *hasn't touched the soup that is in front of him. Everyone else follows his glance towards* **Christian**.

Helge In my eyes, Michael, you don't exactly put me in mind of a lodge brother, but Christian mentioned to Poul that your café has turned the corner.

Christian *nods. A slight pause.*

And since Christian isn't interested in joining, I think you might expect to be invited to join.

Michael *and* **Mette** *are pleased.*

Helge We all need a leg up from time to time, don't we? Perhaps this evening you can act like a normal human being.

Michael *is stung.* **Helge**'s *glance drifts towards* **Pia**.

Helge Perhaps you can keep your hands to yourself. Do you understand me?

Mette *looks at* **Pia** *and then at* **Michael**. *She is unhappy.*

Helge And perhaps tonight you can help smooth things along? We don't want to lump it all on Helmut, do we?

Helmut It's my honour.

Helge   Do you think you can handle that?

Michael   Yes, of course. Can you hurry up? Helmut hasn't got a drink. Poul, would you like a drink?

A slight pause.

Grandfather   I was thinking of saying something later. But it won't be anything for the ears of small girls!

Helene   I'm sure it won't be.

A slight pause.

Michael   Why are you sitting moping, Poul?

Poul   I thought I'd cheered up?

Michael   In my family we prefer jolly guests.

Poul   It was baking in the car on the way up here. I was sweating like a French rapist. I had to take my shirt off. I think I looked quite peculiar sitting in the traffic jam with a bare chest.

Michael   Haven't you got air-conditioning, you silly old sod?

Poul   Yes, but you get so dehydrated. My mouth feels like the inside of a pair of old socks. I have to say, I'm not enjoying the soup.

Michael   You need to drink some water, doesn't he, Mette?

Mette *ignores him.*

Michael   Mette?

Helmut   The lobster soup is delicious.

Poul   It's a salmon soup.

Helene   Is it a salmon soup?

Poul   I'd swear it is.

Helene   It's not, it's lobster.

Helmut   I think it's delicious.

Grandfather   Yes. The tomato soup is terrific.

Helene   It's not tomato soup. It's lobster soup.

Poul   With a mouth like mine it doesn't make much difference.

Christian *taps on his glass and stands.*

Christian   It's seven o'clock. I'd like to make the first toast.

A slight pause.

I think it's my responsibility, as the eldest son, isn't that right, Helmut?

Helmut *nods his assent.*

Helmut   Of course, Christian – please.

Christian   But first I've got a speech I'd like to make, about my father.

Helge *is wary, but smiles.*

Christian   I've written two speeches, actually. You get to choose the one I give. One is green. The other one is yellow.

Christian *holds the two speeches up so that* **Helge** *can see them. There is laughter – especially from* **Poul**. **Kim** *enters.*

Poul   Take the yellow one!

Michael   That's better, you miserable sod!

Helene   Look, he's snapped right out of it now.

Poul   There's nothing like a good trick to liven me up. I like a wheeze. Well done, Christian.

Helge   I'll have the green one.

Pause.

Christian   The green one?

A slight pause.

The green one's a very interesting choice.

Helge   Is it?

A slight pause.

Christian   It's a kind of 'truth' speech.

A slight pause.

I've decided to call it 'When Daddy takes a bath'.

Everyone laughs except **Helge**.

I was very small when we moved here and I loved it. I dare say it was the beginning of a new era for all of us. We had all this space for the first time.

A slight pause.

We had all the room we could wish for. And Linda, my sister, who is now dead – we got up to a lot of trouble tearing around the place.

A slight pause.

Then, as you know, there was a restaurant here – where we are now. I can't think of how many times Linda put something in the food without the guests discovering it. A petal. Something like that.

A slight pause.

We hid and watched them and Linda would scream with delight. And so would I.

A slight pause.

She had the most infectious laugh you can imagine. I can hear her now.

A slight pause.

We never lasted hiding for more than two seconds before we were caught rolling around the floor screaming with laughter. We always got found out. But nothing ever happened.

A slight pause.

Actually, as it turned out, it was much more dangerous when Dad was going to have a bath. I'm not sure if you all remember, but Dad was always taking baths.

Everyone laughs again, but **Helene** *knocks over a glass on the table. Red wine stains the cloth. A slight pause.*

Every time he had a bath, he took Linda and me into his office.

Pause.

There were some things he liked to do first. Like locking the door and pulling the blinds down. Turning the lights off and switching one of the lamps on. Everything had to be just so for him.

A slight pause.

Then he took off his shirt and trousers. We had to do the same. And he lay us down on the green sofa and he raped us. He raped us. He took advantage of us sexually. He had sex with his precious children. I think you threw out the green sofa, didn't you, Dad?

Silence.

A couple of months ago, when Linda died, I realised that my father was a very clean man. I thought this is something I want to share with the rest of my family. I want you to know this about my father. I thought you need to know that.

A slight pause.

Helge is a clean man. A very clean man, my father.

Michael's **Little Girl** *hides under the table.* **Mette** *tries to retrieve her.*

Anyway, we're here to celebrate his sixtieth birthday. Just think what it's like to live a long life. To see your children grow up. Your granddaughter grow up.

A slight pause.

Enough of all that – you're not here to hear me talk all night. We're here to celebrate and I think we should do that. Thanks for all the good years. Congratulations. Happy birthday.

Poul *starts to clap buts stops when* **Michael** *looks at him.*
Christian *remains standing.* **Helge** *looks for* **Lars**. **Kim** *exits.*

Helge   We haven't got anything to drink.

Mette   Out from there, will you!

A slight pause.

Pia, *as stunned as the rest of them, moves to fix drinks. The* **Little Girl** *appears and sits back on her seat.*

Michael   Let's get something in these glasses then, chop-chop.

Suddenly **Grandfather** *taps his glass with his spoon and stands up.* **Christian** *remains on his feet.*

Grandfather   Christian, you were the first to speak but now it's my turn. Else, today is your birthday.

Poul   It's Helge.

Grandfather   What did he say?

Helene   He said that its Helge's birthday today.

Helmut *laughs uneasily.*

Grandfather   Helge, today's your birthday. And I think that's wonderful. You've become a big man over the years. A man who can take a story that's a little bit blue!

Christian   I'm afraid I have to go now.

Grandfather   Where are you going? What are you doing? Sit down. It's my turn.

Christian *exits.*

Grandfather   I remember once when Helge was young he came to me and he said he found it difficult to meet girls.

Helene *taps her glass and gets up.*

Helene   I'm sorry for interrupting.

A slight pause.

I'd just like to say I hope none of you took what Christian said seriously. Seriously. He's my brother and I love him very much.

Helge *nods.*

Helene   But what he said is ludicrous.

A slight pause.

If there had been anything remotely true in what he said I would have known. I'm sorry for interrupting. It's just that I got quite a shock then. I'm sorry.

Helene *sits down and* **Grandfather** *taps his glass again.*

Grandfather   Helge, today's your birthday. You've become a big man over the years. A man who can take a story that's a little bit blue!

Grandfather *taps his glass.*

Else. No Helge. Today is your birthday. You are a big man now. You can handle a story that's a little bit blue, can't you?

Helene   No – Grandad.

Helmut   Have we got to hear this again?

Poul   I'm not sure I can take any more today. Look, it's gone a funny colour I'm sure.

Poul *opens his mouth wide.*

Grandfather   Helge, today is your birthday.

There's some awkward laughter.

Helmut   Oh, not again.

Helene   This is the fourth time!

Helmut   Why don't you let him get it over with?

Grandfather   You're old enough now to take a story that's a little bit blue, aren't you? I remember when Helge was a young man he came to me and he said that he had problems meeting girls.

Helge *nods.*

Grandfather   So I said to him, 'What you need to do my boy is buy a potato and stuff it down your swimming trunks. When you go to the lake to swim with your friends in the summer. Then all of the girls will come running after you.' Well, the summer came, of course, and he comes home – depressed.

Michael   There you go, Poul, you miserable bastard.

Poul   What's that?

Grandfather   And he says nobody would talk to him. So I said to him, 'I can see why boy. You're meant to put the potato down the front of your trunks – not the back – you wally.'

Everyone makes an effort to laugh except **Helge**. **Grandfather** *sits down. Pause.*

Helmut *stands.*

Helmut   Three cheers for Helge! Hip, hip –

All   Hooray!

Helmut   Hip, hip –

All   Hooray!

Helmut   Hip, hip –

All   Hooray!

Christian *enters.* **Helmut** *sings.*

Helmut
   For he's a jolly good fellow

They all sing. **Christian** *sits down and joins in loudly,* **Helene** *avoids his glance.*

There is applause, which dies down as **Christian** *continues to clap.* **Helmut** *sits down. Everyone continues with their meal. Long pause.*

Christian *thinks and then taps his glass and stands up again.*

Christian   I apologise for interrupting again.

A slight pause.

I'm sorry but I've forgotten the most important thing. We're here today because it is my father's birthday – We're not here for any other reason.

A slight pause.

I'm sorry if I led you all up the garden path before. I am sorry. I'd like to make it up to you all now by asking you to charge your glasses. To my father.

Helmut Well done, Christian.

Poul Yes, well done.

Christian If you would all like to stand with me. And raise your glasses.

Everyone stands.

To the man who killed my sister. To a murderer.

Helge *gets up and exits immediately, followed by* **Else**.

Else Helge!

Christian *sits down demonstratively and begins eating his soup.*
Helmut *nervously taps his glass.*

Helmut I'd like to suggest a break here, a cigarette, before the main course?

Mette *gathers the* **Little Girl**. **Lars** *looks for* **Helene**.

Mette Come on! Downstairs now!

Michael What are you doing?

Helene *nods her assent to* **Lars**, *who exits*. **Helmut** *looks for* **Pia**.

Helmut The cigarettes. Chop-chop.

Pia *exits.*

Mette *ignores* **Michael**, *who glares at* **Christian**.

Michael I said, what are you doing?

Michael *catches hold of* **Mette** *but she shakes him off and takes the* **Little Girl** *and exits. Pause.*

Helmut   Poul, why don't you do something?

Poul   I suffer from extreme depressions and this isn't helping me one bit.

Michael   Go on, man. Jesus. Just sing something.

Poul   I think I would like to fetch my coat.

Helmut   No, no, no.

A slight pause.

Michael   There's no need for that. He's fucking crazy. No, we'll break for a smoke and you can sing. Like old times, eh, Poul?

Poul   I think I ought to go.

Michael   No. Not yet.

Helmut   Poul, listen to Michael.

Poul *leaves.* **Michael** *exits after him. A slight pause.*

Helmut *notices* **Grandfather** *hasn't a clue what's happening.*

Helmut   Come on there. I'll help you.

Grandfather   Where are we going now?

Helmut   For a cigar.

Grandfather   Oh, good.

Helmut   This way.

Helmut *and* **Grandfather** *exit. Only* **Helene** *and* **Christian** *remain.*

Helene   Are you insane?

A slight pause.

Can you hear what I'm saying, Christian?

A slight pause.

Are you completely fucking insane?

Christian *doesn't reply.*

Christian!

He continues to slurp his soup and drink. **Helene** *is exasperated and leaves.* **Christian** *is alone at the table. Pause.*

Christian *moves to go.* **Kim** *enters with a bottle of schnapps and a cigarette, smoking.* **Kim** *blocks* **Christian***'s path and puts out his cigarette in a plate of leftover soup.*

Kim   How are you?

Christian   I'm good. I'm fine. I've got to go.

Kim   Well done.

A slight pause.

I heard you.

A slight pause.

Congratulations. You've made your speech and now you're going home. You've lost. Nothing has happened.

Christian   Are you pissed?

Kim   I can't cook otherwise. You know that. How long have we known each other?

Christian   I've got to go now.

Kim   Come on.

A slight pause.

Kim *embraces* **Christian***, squeezes him.*

We started school in the same class, that's right, isn't it? We scrumped apples together. I've been waiting for you to do this ever since then. And now you're running away.

A slight pause.

From your father, who made you and Linda draw straws.

A slight pause.

It was a great touch making him choose. Brilliant. Just like your father did. Well done. I loved that.

Christian What do you want me to do, then?

A slight pause.

Kim Any minute now your father will come and find me
and check on me. To see how things are progressing and
give me a time for the main course. Then he'll say, 'I think
they like the food.' It's always the same, I'll pour him a
schnapps and we'll have a drink together. Like mates.
Always the same; you watch.

Pause.

Christian *sits and thinks.* **Helge** *enters. He smiles at* **Christian**
but turns to **Kim**.

Helge A wonderful first course. I think everyone liked it.

Kim Thank you. I'm pleased you enjoyed it. I was worried
that it might have been a touch cold.

A slight pause.

Helge Let's have a schnapps. The three of us together.
The way we used to have lemonade. When you were little.

Kim Would you like one, Christian?

Christian I'd rather not.

Helge Oh, you don't want to?

A slight pause.

Kim *fixes* **Helge** *a schnapps with his glass.* **Helge** *drinks it
quickly.* **Christian** *returns to his soup.*

Helge It's crap but it tastes good if you know what I
mean. I'd like a few words with my son. In private.

Kim *nods and exits. A slight pause.*

Helge *claps.*

Helge I love speeches.

A slight pause.

But they fade so quickly. How many speeches have you
heard in your life that you can remember?

A slight pause.

Tragical. Comical. Tragical-comical, comical-tragical.
Exceptional. Highly embarrassing in the moment, some of
them.

A slight pause.

But then the moment passes.

A slight pause.

A shame if the speech in question had anything remotely
important to say. How are you?

Christian   I'm fine.

Helge   Are you?

Christian   I'm fine.

Helge   Are you sure?

A slight pause.

I don't really understand anything any more. There must be
something wrong with my mind.

A slight pause.

It must be because I'm getting older.

Pause.

Christian   You shouldn't worry about me.

Helge   But I am.

Christian   I'm just a bit confused lately. You know? Too
much work?

A slight pause.

All that stuff with Linda.

Helge   Yes.

Christian   Just forget it.

A slight pause.

Helge The things you said before. It's serious. You ought to contact the police.

Christian It's nothing. Just forget it. I mean it. You shouldn't even entertain the thought any more.

A slight pause.

I can't sleep. I feel strange. Just forget it. I'm sorry.

A slight pause.

How's everything going in there?

Helge It's going fine. It takes a lot more to shock them than that, don't you worry.

A slight pause.

What is it that you're trying to do to me?

Christian I'd like to sit here on my own. I'd like to be left alone.

Christian *stands and moves to go.*

Helge What would you think if I stood up and said a few words about you?

A slight pause.

A few words about how sick you were as a child. How you always had to destroy everything for your brother and sisters. How you stole their toys from them and burned them while they watched. What a twisted spirit you have and always have had.

Silence.

I could also mention your mother and father having to come to France to try and get you out of the loony bin you ended up in. Your sick mind pouring out while we watched you pumped full of drugs and what an effect it all had on your mother. I could also say how hopeless you are with women. Useless. Beautiful women who you let walk by, year on year, because there's so little man in you, Christian. And of course, I could always talk about your sister.

A slight pause.

Did Linda ever say goodbye to you?

A slight pause.

Was there a letter for you?

A slight pause.

She left letters for the rest of us. Perhaps the reason for that, perhaps the reason for that is that she knew you abandoned her. Like you up and abandoned all of us. As usual.

A slight pause.

I remember the days when she asked for you. Every time the phone rang she thought it was you.

A slight pause.

But it was never you because, as usual, you were only concerned with looking after yourself. And you dare come here tonight and sling your filthy muck at me. At the family that's only ever given, given, given you.

A slight pause.

Your mother doesn't want to see you again.

A slight pause.

But I think you should feel what it's like to have someone spit in your face. Feel what it's like to have your own flesh and blood spit in your face. Of course, you won't. You haven't got the stomach for it.

Christian *hesitates. Pause.*

Have a good trip home. It's good to see you again, son.

Helge *touches* **Christian**'s *cheek. A slight pause.*

They're waiting for me in there.

Helge *exits.* **Christian** *is alone. He is devastated. Long pause.*

Pia *enters. She clears his place. Pause.*

Pia   You fell asleep.

Pia *continues working.*

Are you sleeping?

Pause.

Christian *stands and exits. A slight pause.*

Pia *stops. She is upset. Pause.*

Kim *and* **Lars** *enter. A slight pause.*

Kim   It's Christian's turn tonight.

Lars   Oh no. Please, Kim.

A slight pause.

Kim   Tonight is Christian's turn. No one leaves here until he's done. I mean it. Take their car keys if you have to.

A slight pause.

Pia   Okay.

Pia *giggles.* **Lars** *is concerned.*

Lars   I don't think he intends to say any more now.

Kim   Let's wait and see, shall we?

Pia *smiles at* **Kim**, *trying to encourage him. He relents and nods.*

Kim   Be careful.

Pia *nods.* **Kim** *spots the schnapps. He pours himself a shot. He lifts the glass.*

Kim   To Christian.

Pia   To Christian.

Lars   To Christian.

Kim *gulps down the schnapps in one.*

Blackout.

2.2

Gbatokai *is alone. He's a black man. He looks around.*

Gbatokai   Hello? Hello?

Michael *enters.*

Michael   Hey, what do you want?

Gbatokai   I'm here for the party.

Michael   I think you've come to the wrong place.

Gbatokai   No, I'm in the right place.

Michael   This is a private party. A private party, do you understand me? No gatecrashers, mate?

Gbatokai   I'm invited. My name's Gbatokai.

Lars *enters, busy.*

Michael   Hang on a minute, just a minute, we don't need any music. No band tonight, mate. You'll have to go home.

Gbatokai *shakes his head.* **Mette** *enters with the* **Little Girl**.

Michael   Look, I'll give you five hundred kroner if you piss off now. Go on.

Gbatokai   What?

Michael   Listen, do yourself a favour and leave, will you, mate. If we'd wanted a band we'd have booked one.

Pia *enters, busy.*

Gbatokai   I'm not here to play. I'm invited.

Lars   It's true.

Michael   Listen, you stay out of this.

Lars   He is. He's invited.

Lars *allows himself a small smile and exits.* **Mette** *settles the* **Little Girl** *at the table.*

Gbatokai   You must be Helene's brother?

Michael   Now listen, mate, I don't know how you know my sister and I don't want to know but just get out of my face.

Gbatokai   Excuse me?

Helene *enters. She's overjoyed to see* **Gbatokai**. *She embraces him.* **Lars** *enters. He continues with his work.*

Helene   Hi, baby, I've missed you so much. Come here.

Gbatokai   How are you doing?

Helene   I've missed you so much. I'm so happy you got here.

Pia *exits.* **Helene** *lets go of* **Gbatokai**.

Helene   Michael, what's going on?

Michael   What the fucking hell do you mean?

Gbatokai   He was trying to throw me out.

Helene *throws her arms around* **Gbatokai** *and kisses him.* **Michael** *is shocked and tries to pull them apart. The* **Little Girl** *hides under the table.*

Michael   What the hell do you think you're doing, dragging a fucking monkey to Dad's birthday? Jesus Christ, a bloody monkey. Look at him.

Helene   You don't stand there and call Gbatokai a monkey, you understand me?

Michael   Relax.

Helene   You're fucking sick in the head, you know that, Michael, you fucking Nazi prick!

Michael *catches* **Lars'** *eye.*

Michael   I've got everything under control.

Christian *enters.* **Gbatokai** *looks at* **Christian**.

Gbatokai   Christian?

Christian *notices* **Gbatokai**.

Christian Hi, I'm Christian.

Gbatokai I know.

Christian Make yourself at home. Welcome to this — curious — birthday party.

Mette *is at her wits' end and folds her arms.* **Helene** *sits purposefully guiding* **Gbatokai** *to the seat beside her.* **Lars** *exits.*

Mette Out of there! Now!

The **Little Girl** *sheepishly reappears.* **Poul** *enters.*

Poul You haven't seen my car keys have you?

Silence.

Have you?

Michael No, we haven't, Poul.

Poul I feel on the precipice this evening, you know? Very close to a complete collapse.

Helene Do as you please, Poul.

Poul Thank you for everything.

Helmut *enters with* **Helge**. *He coughs and catches everyone's attention.*

Helmut After that little — what shall we call it? — intermezzo pianissimo, I think we should sit down again, for the main course, don't you?

Helge *nods and walks to his seat.*

Poul You haven't seen my car keys, have you?

Helmut No.

Poul I've had enough now.

Helmut I think you should give things a chance. Don't you think we owe it to our lodge brother, Helge?

Poul Well. I don't know.

Poul *sits. All settle at the table.* **Pia** *enters and stands by* **Lars**, *ready to serve the main course.* **Helge** *stares intently at* **Christian**.

I suffer with extreme depressions and today has not been a good day.

Helmut   Poul, please, be quiet and join in. As it says on Alfred Hitchcock's gravestone, 'This is what happens to small naughty boys'. Helge, you can't avoid the Hansen family traditions, my friend.

Else *and* **Grandfather** *enter.* **Else** *guides him towards his seat.* **Pia** *and* **Lars** *exit.*

Helene   This is my boyfriend, Mum. Gbatokai, this is my mother.

Else *moves to shake his hand.*

Else   Welcome, my dear, welcome.

Gbatokai   Hello.

Else   It's lovely to see you again.

Gbatokai   Excuse me?

Helene   No, Mum, no, I don't think you've met before?

Else   Really?

Helene   That was another one.

Else   It's nice to see you.

Gbatokai   Nice to see you too.

Else *returns to her seat. The silence is awful.* **Helge** *maintains his beady stare at* **Christian**. *Long pause – longer than you think you can get away with.*

Pia *and* **Lars** *enter and begin to serve the main course.* **Michael** *and* **Helmut** *pour drinks.*

Poul   Could you pass the salt and pepper, please?

They begin to eat the meal – in complete silence. **Mette** *watches* **Pia**, **Michael** *watches* **Gbatokai**, **Helene** *watches* **Lars**, **Poul** *watches* **Helmut**, **Grandfather** *watches* **Else**, **Helge** *watches* **Christian**. *After a little while the* **Little Girl** *disappears under the table. And the only sound apart from that of the meal is* *of her giggling and playing under the table.* **Mette** *lets her be. It is unbearable. Again this continues for longer than you think you can get away with.*

Suddenly **Else** *stands.*

Helmut   Well, this family has never been one for maintaining the order of the speeches. But there is still one person who has shown exemplary behaviour at this table. If the birthday boy is my Danish father, Else is my Danish mother. Everybody's mother. Else, the floor is yours.

Helmut *claps and so do the other guests, relieved.*

Else   Thank you, Helmut, thank you all. I would just like to say how much I appreciate it that you've all come here this evening.

A slight pause.

I would like to thank my husband. For the way you've cared for your family, for your zest for life, for the way you love us all. You've given me everything a wife could possibly ask for. Thank you, darling. You've given me thirty-five wonderful years.

A slight pause.

I'd also like to take the opportunity to say something to my three children. It's fantastic to see all the things that you've accomplished. Michael, little Michael, we haven't seen much of you lately. First there was boarding school, then the school ship and catering college in Switzerland.

A slight pause.

It's a shame you didn't become a chef – but there's still time.

Else *laughs, somehow she manages to warm the room.*

At least, you've given us, with little Mette, a wonderful granddaughter. Thank you.

The **Little Girl** *pops out from the table and startles* **Else**. **Helene** *laughs with her mother.*

Helene, you're the − eccentric one − my dear. I really mean that, dear. First of all you said you were going to be in a rock band. And then you joined the Young Socialists. You always said to us you wanted to follow your own star. And so you have. We're thrilled you ended up in anthropology − though your father and I were hoping for law.

Everyone except **Christian** *and* **Helge** *laughs.*

I can't recall now the number of poor countries whose unfortunate inhabitants have had to cope with you.

Else *takes a sip of her water.*

Speaking of which, I would like to welcome Gonzalez.

Helene   Gbatokai, Mum.

Else   Welcome, Kai, I do apologise.

A slight pause.

And you, Christian − my dear.

Christian *downs his wine.*

You have always been one of a kind, a really creative little boy. I've always thought there's a wonderful writer inside you. Hidden away.

A slight pause.

When Christian was little he had an imaginary friend. Snoot. They agreed on everything. If Snoot didn't like something then neither did Christian.

A slight pause.

But, darling, it's important now to be able to separate fantasy from reality.

A slight pause.

I understand that you're angry with your father. I've been angry with your father before as well.

A slight pause.

But it's something you should deal with in private. Perhaps the things you said earlier were a little bit over the top.

Else *smiles.*

I think that you've been playing with Snoot today, Christian. I think you've both upset your father very much. I think you should stand up and say sorry. It won't do any harm.

A slight pause.

Christian, would you please stand up.

Everyone waits but **Christian** *is paralysed. Long pause.*

Michael   Stand up, Christian.

Long pause.

Christian *takes a gulp of another drink, taps his glass and stands.* **Else** *sits.* **Helge** *maintains his stare as he has throughout.*

Christian   Okay, I'm sorry for interrupting yet again. Ah, you see.

A slight pause.

In 1980 you, my mother, came into the office and you saw me kneeling. You saw your husband without his trousers on. I'm sorry that you saw your son like that. I'm sorry that your husband told you to get out. I'm sorry that you did what he asked without a second thought. I'm sorry that you're so deceitful and rotten that I hope you die from it. And I'm sorry that you fat pigs, the lot of you, just sit there and calmly listen to her hypocritical crap.

Michael *gets up and walks towards* **Christian**. *The* **Little Girl** *hides under the table.* **Pia** *is frozen.*

Christian   And I'm sorry that your husband – for thirty-five years! /

Michael   Come on. Come with me now. /

Christian   Can I finish speaking? Can I please finish speaking? /

Helmut *stands.*

Helmut Let's go, Christian. /

Michael Take it easy. It's over now. Let's go outside. /

Michael *grasps his brother's arm.*

Christian Let go of me. /

Michael No, you're going out! /

Helmut *grabs* **Christian** *from the other side. They try to drag him away.* **Christian** *fights.*

Christian I just want to say one more thing! /

Gbatokai *stands.*

Gbatokai What are you doing? /

Christian You were at boarding school. /

Michael Keep your nose out! /

Helene Michael, what are you going to do? /

Christian You don't know shit about anything! /

Gbatokai What are you going to do? Tuck him in? Kiss him good night? I don't think so!

Michael *lets go of* **Christian** *and heads towards* **Gbatokai**.

Christian But you all know the same, don't you? /

Michael Have you got a problem? /

Christian You know it's true! /

Helene Don't, Michael! Don't, Michael, please! Michael!

Michael *pushes* **Gbatokai**. **Mette** *taps her glass and stands. She begins to sing quietly, in Danish, a sweet, peaceful old song.* **Michael** *turns back towards* **Mette** *and then* **Christian**.

Mette
There is idyllic peace in the lonely woods
And the longing of the heart ceases here
Where peace and resting are

Christian You know it's true don't you?

Mette
Hear the church bells ring in the evening calm
The robin's last chirps before he dozes off
By the lake a frog croaks loudly
As the fog rolls over field and stream

The two men really get hold of **Christian** *now and try harder than ever to drag him from the room.* **Helge** *comforts his wife. They turn away from the table.* **Poul** *decides to continue with his meal.*

And the bells cease their ringing
And evening's calm settles over us all.

Christian   Don't you, Michael?

Christian *gets away from* **Michael** *and returns to his seat. He sits, taps his glass with a fork and then stands again.*

Sorry, where were we? Ah, yes, yes. Don't you, Mummy – my trusty witness?

Michael *and* **Helmut** *go towards* **Christian**.

In 1980 you came into the office and you saw my father's cock in front of my mouth, you fucking bitch, you bitch, you fucking bitch!

Gbatokai *lifts his glass. The two men struggle even harder to get* **Christian** *out and he fights even harder.*

Gbatokai   To your brother.

Michael *spits at* **Gbatokai**.

Here's to your brother!

Michael *lets go as* **Helmut** *gets* **Christian** *out of the room.*

To your brother.

Helene   Stop it, please, Michael!

Michael   Why don't you get up and make a speech then, eh?

Gbatokai   What?

Mette   Michael, enough!

Michael   Speech!

Gbatokai   Don't tempt me, you fuck!

Michael *downs a glass of wine and starts to loudly sing an old Danish children's song which is used as a racist taunt.*

Michael
    I've seen a little sambo man –

Grandfather *joins* **Michael** *as he recognises the song.* **Else** *turns and sings too.*

Singers
    With a face as black as a frying pan –

Gbatokai   What is this? /

Singers
    He said so many funny things –

Helene   It's a fucking racist song. /

Singers
    And in his nose was a great big ring –

Gbatokai   I know what it is! /

Singers
    He laughed at me and said these words –

Gbatokai   Fuck you! /

Singers
    And I didn't understand a single thing
    Hullah hut hottentot
    Hulla hopsa sambo man.

Gbatokai *goes to* **Michael**. *They push each other and begin to fight. It's stupid and brutal and involves lots of pushing.* **Helene** *screams and holds her head.* **Pia** *goes to her and holds her.*

Helene   I can't stand this any more!

Pia   Easy.

The fighting men crash into the table. **Poul** *continues to eat.* **Else** *screams.*

Helene   They're going to kill each other!

Pia   Come with me.

Helene   I just want to go home, I really want to go home now.

Helene *rests her head on the table.* **Christian** *comes back in followed by* **Helmut**, *who beckons* **Michael**. **Michael** *sees him and scrambles away from* **Gbatokai**. **Helmut** *and* **Michael** *drag* **Christian** *out. Pause.*

Helene   My head hurts. It's killing me. Pia, there are some tablets in my bag. Can you get them for me?

Pia *looks at* **Helene** *and then exits. A slight pause.*

Gbatokai *stands.* **Grandfather** *looks at him and raises his glass.*

Grandfather   Cheers.

Poul   Cheers.

Else *exits.*

Helge   Else!

Helge *watches her go. Pause.*

Poul *notices. He taps his glass and stands. The* **Little Girl** *emerges from under the table.*

Poul   Helge, as you can see, I haven't left yet. And you know what? I'm not going!

Christian *enters, chased by* **Helmut** *and* **Michael**. *They exit.*

A slight pause.

I will be with you until the end. It's been a wonderful dinner. And a really lively party so far! Thank you, my brother. Thank you.

Helge   Thank you.

Poul *raises his glass and downs his wine.* **Helge** *stands and leaves. The* **Little Girl** *chases after him.*

3.1

Michael *and* **Helmut** *drag* **Christian** *into a clearing in the forest.* **Christian** *struggles and fights vigorously.*

Michael   It's over now!

Helmut   Haven't you had enough now?

Helmut *lets go of* **Christian**.

Michael   No!

Helmut *advances.*

He's my brother, no!

Helmut   Where shall we put him?

Michael   Over there.

Helmut   Where?

Michael   Get rid of him.

Helmut   What do you mean?

Michael   Leave him here.

Christian *really struggles to get free.*

Do we really have to tie you up!

Helmut   Come on!

Helmut *holds* **Christian** *as* **Michael** *ties his hands.*

Michael   Why did you do it? Why did you say that shit? Why did you do it?

Christian   You weren't there.

Michael   No, it's shit.

Christian   You were away!

Michael   Shut up!

Christian   You were away at school!

Michael *slaps* **Christian**.

Helmut   Is he tied up yet?

Michael   Nearly.

Helmut   Calm down now.

Michael   Easy now.

Christian *howls with frustration.*

Take it easy, Christian.

Christian *spits in* **Michael**'s *face.* **Michael** *attacks his brother savagely.* **Helmut** *tries to pull them apart as they fight.*

Helmut   Leave him, just leave him!

Helmut *manages to pull* **Michael** *away.* **Christian** *lies on the ground groaning. His hands are free but he is hurt.* **Helmut** *exits.* **Michael** *looks at his brother one more time and exits. Pause.*

Christian *sits up, his nose is bleeding. He considers the forest. He thinks he hears something. A slight pause.*

Pia *enters* **Helene**'s *room and looks for her bag.*

Christian   Who's that?

A slight pause.

Who's there? Is that you, Michael?

A slight pause.

Linda?

Christian *slowly comes to his feet.* **Pia** *spots* **Helene**'s *bag and rifles through it.*

Linda?

Christian *breaks into a broad smile. Tears run down his cheeks.* **Pia** *finds the tablets and opens the tube. The letter* **Helene** *hid there falls out. A slight pause.*

A cool white light soaks them. **Christian** *looks to one side.* **Pia** *reads the letter.*

Christian   What is it?

A slight pause.

Come here.

Christian *closes his eyes. A slight pause.*

A shadow falls across them. **Christian** *notices* **Pia**. *She slowly moves towards him.*

I saw her out in the woods.

A slight pause.

I saw Linda.

Pia   No. She's dead.

Christian   Dead, dead, dead.

A slight pause.

My sister is dead.

Pia   Christian?

Christian   Did you manage to take care of the pudding?

Pia *shakes her head.*

Christian   Oh. Shame. I thought I saw you in the woods.

Pia   Did you?

Christian   What's happening? I can't stop it. It won't stop. It only stops when the sun comes up. I like it.

Pia *smiles.*

Christian   I love you.

Pia *thinks. She passes* **Christian** *the letter. He reads it.*

3.2

Gbatokai *kisses and comforts* **Helene**. **Pia** *watches them as she busies herself at the dining table.* **Helene** *looks at* **Gbatokai**.

Gbatokai   Everything will work out fine. I know it will. I can feel it.

Helene   I don't know. I really want to go home now.

Gbatokai   Trust me.

Helene   Are you sure?

Gbatokai   I swear.

Christian *enters. He is dazed and walking slowly.* **Helene** *is surprised.* **Gbatokai** *smiles.*

Christian, my man.

A slight pause.

Helene   Christian?

Christian   What time is it?

Helene   I don't know where Michael is.

A slight pause.

Christian *gives* **Helene** *the letter. A slight pause.*

Christian   You dropped something. You should be more careful.

Helene   Christian?

Helene *looks at the letter and crushes it in her hand. The sound of the Danish birthday song, which we heard earlier, is audible. A conga snakes into the room.* **Helmut** *leads,* **Helge** *is behind, then* **Else**, *then the* **Little Girl**, *then* **Mette**, *then* **Poul**, *then* **Grandfather**, *then* **Michael** *and finally* **Lars**. **Christian** *moves into the shadows.*

All
   It's Daddy's birthday
   Oh yes it is and it is today

It's Daddy's birthday
Oh yes it is and it is today
And now you'll hear how loud we whistle
And now you'll hear how loud we whistle

As they whistle loudly and the song comes to a rousing finale, the conga disintegrates. The **Little Girl** *runs to* **Helene**. *Everyone is laughing and out of breath.*

Helge   Well, well, well, you've still got it after all these years.

Helmut   I can keep going for longer than you think, Helge.

There's general laughter.

Else   You're not going, are you?

Helene   Yes.

Else   No, don't go.

Helene   I want to go home.

Else   We came to find you. You mustn't go. They must stay! It's time for pudding.

Helge *nods his assent.* **Gbatokai** *glances in* **Christian**'s *direction.*

Helmut   I love the traditions here. Dancing round the house. I love it.

Poul   This is the party that never ends!

A slight pause.

It really doesn't end! Ha, ha.

Helmut *is wary, but then smiles, when he spots something at his place.*

Helmut   I love these family traditions. Look! After the dance a note appears on the toastmaster's glass. And there it is!

Helmut *reaches for the glass, which he taps with a spoon and then looks at the note.*

'A certain man urges his sister to read a letter to her father.'

Everyone laughs and applauds except **Helene**, **Gbatokai**, **Pia** *and* **Michael**. **Helmut** *nods towards* **Michael**.

Helmut   Are you feeling shy Helene? Well, it's kind of your brother to get you started.

Michael *smiles, when* **Else** *glances at him.*

Well, it seems there's peace in the family again. So let's all give Helene a hand.

Everyone claps.

Michael   Go on, Helene.

Poul   Go on then, dear.

Grandfather   Don't be shy.

Helene tries to leave but **Poul** *stops her.*

Helene *opens the letter crushed in her palm.* **Helene** *looks at* **Gbatokai**. **Christian** *emerges from the shadows.* **Michael** *moves towards him.*

Helge   Ignore him, Michael.

Michael *retreats.* **Helene** *trembles, she is on the verge of cracking.*

Helene   It's. Um. This is from my sister.

A slight pause.

'To the person who finds this letter.'

A slight pause.

'You are most likely to be my brother or my sister. You two have always been good at playing "Getting Hotter, Getting Colder", I know.'

A slight pause.

'I know it must be horrible to find me like this in the bath. But it's okay for me now. Christian and Michael and Helene, I know you're happy in your own ways. You're wonderful.'

A slight pause.

'I love all of you.'

A slight pause.

'I don't want you to think about me like this.'

A slight pause.

'Christian, my darling, darling brother, you have always been with me. Thank you. Thank you for everything. I don't want you to be upset. I love you so much. I don't want you to be involved in this.'

A slight pause.

'And you, Helene. And you, Michael. You're mad, you know that?'

Helene *finds the next very hard indeed.*

'Dad has started to take me again. In my dreams anyway.'

A slight pause.

'I can't go on any more. I need to go away. I've wanted to do it before. I should have done it before.'

A slight pause.

'I know what I'm going to do will hurt you, Christian. I don't want to. I've tried to ring you but you're busy. Please don't feel bad about me. I think it will be lovely on the other side. I'm looking forward to it now. Of course, I'm a little bit frightened to leave without you. I don't want to leave without you. I love you always and for ever.'

A slight pause.

'Linda.'

Christian *stands and comes forward. Pause.*

Helge   That was a beautiful letter. Thank you, my girl. Can you fetch me a glass of port for my daughter? I'd like to drink to her.

A slight pause.

Helge *looks for* **Pia**.

Can you pour some port for my daughter? I'd like to raise my glass to her. I'd like to give her a drink.

Helge *looks for* **Lars**.

Can you get a glass of port for my daughter? I'd like to raise my glass to her. I want to raise my glass to her.

Lars *doesn't move.* **Helge** *looks to* **Pia** *again.* **Helge** *becomes mad with rage.*

Pour some port for my daughter! Fetch the bottle up for my daughter! Can't one of you respect my wishes and do as I ask?

Else *is stiff and helpless.*

Is anyone listening to me? What are you staring at, you fools? Is it my fault that I was given such useless brats?

Pause.

Christian   Somehow, I've never understood why you did it.

Pause.

I've never understood why you did it.

Pause.

Helge   It was all you were good for.

Silence.

Helmut   I have to say it's been a demanding responsibility being the master of ceremonies this evening. I have to say it's my first time.

Helge *moves into the shadows.* **Else** *follows him.*

This is all very moving. I believe we are all deeply moved. Nevertheless I think it's my duty to suggest coffee, perhaps, a little music and a cigar?

Helge's *words hit* **Christian** *with the force of a baseball bat. He faints. The piano plays.*

Helmut *comes forward.* **Pia** *rushes to* **Christian**. **Helmut** *looks for the other guests but no one is listening any more.* **Michael** *looks for* **Helge**. **Grandfather** *is lost.* **Gbatokai** *and* **Helene**

slow dance. **Poul** *searches for his car keys.* **Mette** *packs her case.*
The **Little Girl** *plays.* **Christian** *wakes and crawls towards her.*
Michael *spots* **Helge**.

Michael   Open the door!

Mette *bursts into tears.* **Helene** *stops dancing to comfort her.*

Pia   You're going to bed now.

Christian   I love you.

Michael   It's the fucking postman!

A cool white light soaks them all. **Christian** *looks at the* **Little**
Girl.

Christian   Shall I come with you?

The **Little Girl** *shakes her head.*

Christian   I miss you too.

A shadow falls across them all. **Michael** *discovers* **Helge**. *A slight*
pause.

Michael *launches at* **Helge**. **Christian** *stands.* **Michael** *hits*
him again and again.

Michael   Get down! You fucking get down! Down there!
Down!

Else   Michael, stop it!

He forces **Helge** *to the floor.* **Else** *looks for* **Christian**.

Michael   You stay! I'm sick of your shit. I'm sick of your
lies. You'll never see my daughter again. Never. You
understand that? Never! You bastard, you bastard, you stay
down there! Do as I say! Little Michael's telling you now!
Do as I say!

Else   Christian! He mustn't! He mustn't!

Michael   It's me ringing the doorbell! Me!

Christian *approaches.* **Michael** *kicks his father.* **Helge** *screams*
and cries with fear. **Michael** *unbuttons his fly to try to piss on*
Helge.

Christian   Leave him, Michael. Leave him be.

Christian *pulls* **Michael** *away.*

Helge   You're killing me! You're killing me!

Christian *goes to his father and helps him to his feet.* **Helge** *looks at* **Christian** *and then* **Michael**. **Helge** *exits. A slight pause.*

Christian *and* **Michael** *look at each other.*

3.3

Christian, **Mette**, **Michael**, **Poul**, **Gbatokai** *and* **Helene** *sit for breakfast at the dining table. The* **Little Girl** *helps* **Lars** *and* **Pia** *set the table.*

Lars   Well done, good work.

Mette   Slowly!

Lars   We need the cheese on the table and the marmalade.

The **Little Girl** *runs off.*

Poul   Is there any chance of a little tipple?

Pia   If you would like one.

Poul   Isn't it colder today?

Pia   I don't think so.

Poul   It'll warm me up. A good way to start the day. I think my toes are going to drop off. Morning, all.

Michael   Morning.

Poul   Morning, Christian.

Michael   Morning, Christian.

Christian   Morning.

Michael   How are you?

Christian   Fine.

A slight pause.

Mette   Have a roll.

Poul   Michael, I've been meaning to ask you, where do you buy your pre-wrinkled clothes?

Michael   At Naestved. Could you pass me the butter, please?

Gbatokai *passes* **Michael** *the butter.*

Thank you.

A slight pause.

Where's Grandad?

Christian   He's asleep.

Pause.

The **Little Girl** *comes back in with marmalade.* **Pia** *hovers by* **Christian**. *The* **Little Girl** *places the marmalade on the table and takes her picture book.*

Come and live with me in Paris.

Pia *nods.*

Pia   Yes.

Christian   That's all I want to say.

Pia *smiles and continues.*

Michael   Are you chatting up the staff?

Mette   Shut up, Michael.

Helene   Eat your eggs.

Helge *and* **Else** *enter. They walk past the guests. Silence.*

Else   Morning.

Poul   Morning.

Michael   Morning.

Mette   Morning.

Helene   Morning.

Helge   Morning. Morning, everyone. Bon appétit.

Helge *and* **Else** *sit. The* **Little Girl** *runs to them and she jumps on to* **Helge***'s lap with her picture book.* **Mette** *stands.*

Michael   Come here. Come to your dad.

Helge *lifts the* **Little Girl** *from his lap.*

Helge   I'm sure your father can read that for you.

The **Little Girl** *runs to* **Michael**. **Helge** *taps his glass with a teaspoon and stands.*

I know this is hardly an appropriate time in the middle of breakfast but I will keep things as brief as I can.

A slight pause.

I know when you pack up your things and leave here today it will be the last time I see you.

A slight pause.

I also know now what I've done to my children. It's unforgivable. I know that you all hate me, especially my children. But I would still like you to know, I would still like to say to you, you will always be my children and I will always love you. No matter where you are in the world or what you're doing, you will be in my mind and my heart.

A slight pause.

To you, Christian, I want to say, well done. Well fought, my boy.

Michael *stands and goes to* **Helge**.

Michael   Nice speech, Dad. Well done you. But we'd like to eat now. I think you should disappear now, don't you? We'd like to have our breakfast.

Helge   Yes, yes, of course, of course.

Helge *stands and turns to* **Else**.

Do you want to – Are you coming?

Else   I'll stay here.

Helge *walks back out past the guests.* **Christian** *stands.* **Helge** *exits. They all continue with their breakfast. Silence.*

Christian *sits.* **Pia** *and,* **Lars** *continue to serve, helped by the* **Little Girl**.

Fade.

Methuen Film titles include

The Wings of the Dove
Hossein Armini

Mrs Brown
Jeremy Brock

Persuasion
Nick Dear after Jane Austen

The Gambler
Nick Dear after Dostoyevski

Beautiful Thing
Jonathan Harven

Little Voice
Mark Herman

The Long Good Friday
Barrie Keeffe

State and main
David Mamet

The Crucible
Arthur Miller

The English Patient
Anthony Minghella

The Talented Mr Ripley
Anthony Minghella

Twelfth Night
Trevor Nunn after Shakespeare

The Krays
Philip Ridley

The Reflecting Skin & The Passion of Darkly Noon
Philip Ridley

Trojan Eddie
Billy Roche

Sling Blade
Billy Bob Thornton

The Acid House
Irvine Welsh

Methuen Modern Plays

include work by

Edward Albee
Jean Anouilh
John Arden
Margaretta D'Arcy
Peter Barnes
Sebastian Barry
Brendan Behan
Dermot Bolger
Edward Bond
Bertolt Brecht
Howard Brenton
Anthony Burgess
Simon Burke
Jim Cartwright
Caryl Churchill
Noël Coward
Lucinda Coxon
Sarah Daniels
Nick Darke
Nick Dear
Shelagh Delaney
David Edgar
David Eldridge
Dario Fo
Michael Frayn
John Godber
Paul Godfrey
David Greig
John Guare
Peter Handke
David Harrower
Jonathan Harvey
Iain Heggie
Declan Hughes
Terry Johnson
Sarah Kane
Charlotte Keatley
Barrie Keeffe
Howard Korder

Robert Lepage
Doug Lucie
Martin McDonagh
John McGrath
Terrence McNally
David Mamet
Patrick Marber
Arthur Miller
Mtwa, Ngema & Simon
Tom Murphy
Phyllis Nagy
Peter Nichols
Sean O'Brien
Joseph O'Connor
Joe Orton
Louise Page
Joe Penhall
Luigi Pirandello
Stephen Poliakoff
Franca Rame
Mark Ravenhill
Philip Ridley
Reginald Rose
Willy Russell
Jean-Paul Sartre
Sam Shepard
Wole Soyinka
Shelagh Stephenson
Peter Straughan
C. P. Taylor
Theatre de Complicite
Theatre Workshop
Sue Townsend
Judy Upton
Timberlake Wertenbaker
Roy Williams
Snoo Wilson
Victoria Wood